Jean-Charles V

Agrégé in Hist

Louis IX

Royal Genealogy and A Chronological Look at the History of France

Henri IV

Illustrations by Editions Gisserot
Photographs by Jean-Paul Gisserot
and Christophe Renault
Translation by Angela Moyon

Louis XIV

Louis XVI

Napoléon I

Napoléon III

Front cover: Versailles, Napoleon, Henri IV, the Invalides, the Pont du Gard, Louis XIV.
Back cover: The Conciergerie, the mausoleum of Louis XVI and Marie-Antoinette in Saint-Denis, the Eiffel Tower, the Louvre, Château-Gaillard at Les Andelys, the Arc de Triomphe.

EDITIONS JEAN-PAUL GISSEROT
10, rue Gracieuse - 75005 Paris

Kings, Heads of State and French political regimes

MEROVINGIAN DYNASTY

Clovis I	c. 481-511
Chlotar I	511-561
Chlotar II	584-629
Dagobert I	629-639
"The Sluggard Kings"	639-751

CAROLINGIAN DYNASTY

Pepin the Short	751-768
Carloman	768-771
Charlemagne	768-814
Louis I the Pious	814-840
Charles II the Bald	840-877
Louis II the Stammerer	877-879
Louis III	879-882
Carloman	879-884
Charles the Fat	885-887
Eudes (Robertian)	888-898
Charles III the Simple	893-923
Robert I	922-923
Rudolph (Robertian)	923-936
Louis IV from Overseas	936-954
Lothair	954-986
Louis V the Do-Nothing	986-987

CAPETIAN DYNASTY

Hugh Capet	987-996
Robert II the Pious	996-1031
Henry I	1031-1060
Philip I	1060-1108
Louis VI the Fat	1108-1137
Louis VII the Younger	1137-1180
Philip II Augustus	1180-1223
Louis VIII the Lion	1223-1226
Louis IX (St. Louis)	1226-1270
Philip III the Bold	1270-1285
Philip IV the Fair	1285-1314
Louis X the Stubborn	1314-1316
John I	1316
Philip V the Long	1316-1322
Charles IV the Fair	1322-1328
Philip VI de Valois	1328-1350
John II the Good	1350-1364
Charles V the Wise	1364-1380
Charles VI the Mad	1380-1422
Charles VII	1422-1461
Louis XI	1461-1483
Charles VIII	1483-1498
Louis XII	1498-1515
François I	1515-1547
Henri II	1547-1559
François II	1559-1560
Charles IX	1560-1574
Henri III	1574-1589
Henri IV	1589-1610
Louis XIII	1610-1643
Louis XIV	1643-1715
Louis XV	1715-1774
Louis XVI	1774-1792

c. 481

Middle Ages

1498

Modern France

1789

FIRST REPUBLIC: 1792-1799

CONSULATE: 1799-1804

FIRST EMPIRE

Napoleon I	1804-1814 / 1815

RESTORATION

Louis XVIII	1814-1815 / 1815-1824
Charles X	1824-1830

JULY MONARCHY

Louis-Philippe I	1830-1848

SECOND REPUBLIC

Louis-Napoleon Bonaparte	1848-1852

SECOND EMPIRE :

Napoléon III	1852-1870

THIRD REPUBLIC

Adolphe Thiers	1871-1873
Mac-Mahon	1873-1879
Jules Grévy	1879-1887
Sadi Carnot	1887-1894
Jean Casimir-Périer	1894-1895
Félix Faure	1895-1899
Émile Loubet	1899-1906
Armand Fallières	1906-1913
Raymond Poincaré	1913-1920
Paul Deschanel	1920
Alexandre Millerand	1920-1924
Gaston Doumergue	1924-1931
Paul Doumer	1931-1932
Albert Lebrun	1932-1940

FRENCH STATE (Vichy regime)

Philippe Pétain	1940-1944

PROVISIONAL GOVERNMENT

1944-1947

FOURTH REPUBLIC

Vincent Auriol	1947-1954
René Coty	1954-1959

FIFTH REPUBLIC

Charles de Gaulle	1959-1969
Georges Pompidou	1969-1974
Valéry Giscard d'Estaing	1974-1981
François Mitterrand	1981-1995
Jacques Chirac	1995-

Revolution Empire

1815

19th century

1914

20th century

Prehistory

c. 1 800 000 BC :	Man is known to have been lived on French territory; Palaeolithic Era.
c. 1 200 000 BC :	Beginning of major Ice Age.
c. 1 000 000 BC :	Homo erectus arrives on French territory.
c. 500 000 BC :	Man learns to use fire.
c. 320 000 BC :	Homo erectus is present in Tautavel.
c. 100 000 BC :	Neanderthal Man (La Chapelle-aux-Saints).
c. 30 000 BC :	Modern man (Homo sapiens sapiens or Cro-Magnon Man) lives on French territory.
c. 20 000 BC :	Cave art reaches its apogee. The cave at Lascaux is decorated.
c. 10 000 BC :	End of the last major Ice Age.
c. 9 000 BC :	Beginning of climatic warming.
c. 6 000 BC :	Start of the Stone Age. Man becomes a sedentary farmer. Pottery comes into use.
c. 4 500 - 2 000 BC:	Megalithic culture (dolmens, standing stones).

Kermario Alignment, Carnac (Morbihan). ▲

▲ Main roof in the Rouffignac Cave in Dordogne (Photo by Plassard).

Kerguntuil Dolmen (Côtes d'Armor). ▲

Passage grave I in Liscuit (Côtes d'Armor). ▲

Antiquity

c. 3 500 BC :	Start of the Copper Age.
c. 2 000 BC :	Start of the Bronze Age.
c. 700 – 400 BC :	Celtic invasion of Gaul.
c. 600 BC:	The Phocaeans found Marseille.
125 – 122 BC :	The Romans conquer Provence. Aix-en-Provence is founded.
118 BC :	The Romans found the town of Narbonne.
58 – 50 BC :	The "Gallic Wars". Caesar, a Roman Consul, conquers the entire country of Gaul.
In 52 B.C	He forces Vercingetorix to capitulate in Alesia.
43 BC :	The Romans found Lyon, the administrative capital of the three Gauls.
16 BC :	The Romans build the "Maison carrée" (temple) in Nîmes.
c. 25 AD :	The Romans build the arena in Arles.
48 AD :	Gauls are admitted to the Roman Senate (Claudian Tables).
c. 50 AD :	The Pont du Gard (aqueduct) is built by the Romans.
c. 60 – 70 AD :	The Romans build the arena in Nîmes.
177 AD :	Christians are persecuted and St. Blandine dies a martyr's death in Lyon. Further persecutions take place in 257-258 and 303-304.
212 AD :	An edict handed down by Caracalla grants Roman citizenship to all free men in the Empire.
253 AD :	The Franks and Alemanni invade Gaul (further invasions occur in 256, 260, 270 and 274-275).
260 AD :	A Gallic Empire is founded by Postumus (the secession lasts until 274 AD).
313 AD :	The Roman Emperor, Constantine, promulgates the Edict of Milan, granting religious tolerance and, therefore, the right to practise Christian worship.
c. 352 AD :	The Alemanni and Franks invade Gaul. They are defeated by the future Roman emperor, Julian, in 357-358.
371-397 AD :	St. Martin, Bishop of Tours, spreads Christianity throughout Gaul.
early 5th century :	The Roman Empire is subjected to major invasions by Vandals, Alanni, Suevi, Visigoths, Burgundians and Franks who ravage Gaul before colonising it.
mid 5th century :	The Bretons settle in Armorica.
451 AD :	The Huns invade Gaul, led by Attila. St. Genevieve leads resistance in Paris. Attila is defeated at the Battle of the Catalaunian Fields.
c. 455-470 AD :	The Alemanni settle in Alsace.
476 AD :	The last Roman emperor is removed from power. End of the Roman Empire in the Western World.

The Maison carrée in Nîmes (Gard). ▲

The triumphal arch in Orange (Vaucluse). ▲

The Dark Ages and Middle Ages

A recumbent statue of Childebert I holding a model of Saint-Germain-des-Prés, in Saint-Denis basilica (Seine-Saint-Denis). ▲

The Merovingians

c. 481	:	Accession of Clovis I, King of the Salian Franks from Tournai.
c. 486	:	Clovis I defeats Syagrius, the last representative of Rome in Gaul, at Soissons.
c. 493	:	Clovis I marries Clotilda. He is baptised in Reims c. 498.
c. 496	:	Clovis I defeats the Alemanni at Tolbiac.
507	:	Clovis I defeats the Visigoths at Vouillé.
c. 510	:	The Franks introduce the Salic Law (legal code).
511	:	Death of King Clovis I and division of the kingdom between his four sons.
c. 540	:	St. Benedict of Nursia draws up his Rule (the Benedictine Rule).
558-561	:	The unity of the Frankish kingdom is re-established under Chlotar I.
567 onwards	:	Gradual creation of the three kingdoms of Austrasia, Neustria and Burgundy.
573-594	:	Bishop Gregory of Tours writes his Historia francorum.
c. 585	:	The tithe is introduced.
613	:	Chlotar II rebuilds the unity of the Frankish kingdom. He designates a Mayor of the Palace to head each of the three kingdoms.
639	:	Death of King Dagobert I. Start of the period known as the era of the "Sluggard Kings".
732	:	Charles Martel, Mayor of the Palace, stops the Saracen advance at Poitiers.
751	:	Pepin the Short, Mayor of the Palace, deposes the last Merovingian king, Childeric III, and has himself elected King of the Franks.

The Merovingians

This was the first dynasty of Frankish kings and it reigned over Gaul from 481 to 751 A.D. It is named after Merovech, Clovis' grandfather. The founder of the dynasty is Clovis I, king from 481 to 511 A.D, who was the first king of all the Franks.

In line with Germanic tradition, the kingdom was divided between his heirs on his death and, over the 6th century, three kingdoms were gradually created – Neustria, Austrasia and Burgundy. A long era of conflict ensued and the kingdom of the Franks enjoyed unity only for a few brief periods, under Chlotar I (558-561), Chlotar II (613-629) and Dagobert I (632-639).

From 639 A.D. onwards, the Merovingian monarchy fell into a swift decline and real power passed into the hands of the Mayors of the Palace; this was the period of the "Sluggard Kings". Eventually, in 751 A.D, Pepin the Short, Mayor of the Palace, deposed the last Merovingian sovereign, Childeric III, and seized the throne. This marked the end of the first royal dynasty. ■

A Merovingian belt buckle from La Roche-sur-Foron, Haute-Savoie. Musée d'Art et d'Histoire, Chambéry (Savoie). ▲

Death of Brunehault in 613 A.D. ▲

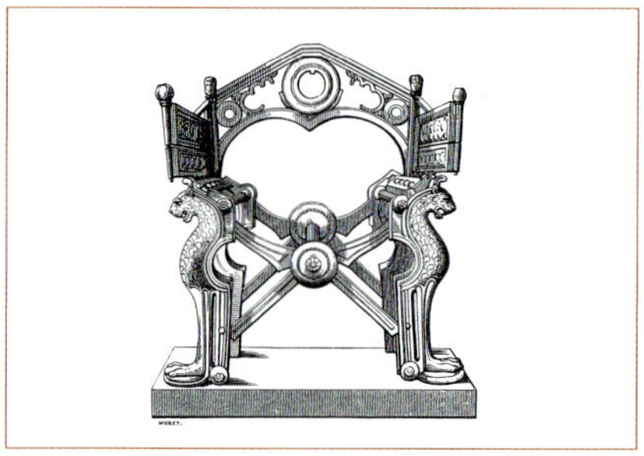

Dagobert's carved bronze throne (c. 630 A.D.). ▲

The Battle of Poitiers in 732 A.D. ▲

Clovis I (c. 466-511), King of the Franks (c. 481-511)

Clovis, son of Childeric I and Basina, succeeded his father as King of the Salian Franks in Tournai c. 481 A.D. Much of his reign was spent in fighting to extend his kingdom. He defeated Syagrius, the last representative of Rome in Gaul, near Soissons in 486 A.D, defeated the Alemanni in Tolbiac in 496 A.D, conquered the King of the Burgundians, Gundobad, near Dijon in 500 A.D. and defeated and killed Alaric II, King of the Visigoths, in Vouillé in 507 A.D. He gradually unified the kingdom of the Franks and extended it to almost all of Gaul, from the Pyrenees to the Rhine. In 493 A.D, Clovis married a Catholic Burgundian princess, Clotilda, thereby obtaining support from the bishops. Under his wife's influence, Clovis had himself baptised with several thousand of his soldiers (c. 498 A.D.). His conversion brought him the support of the Catholics who saw him as the only legitimate king and he then instigated policies that brough him close to the Church. Clovis was not only the conqueror of the Aryans; he was also the protector of new monasteries (St. Genevieve's Abbey). On his death in 511 A.D, his kingdom was divided between his four sons, in accordance with Germanic tradition.

The Merovingians

- **CLOVIS I** (c. 466-511) King of the Franks c. 481 to 511
  - married (1) a Rhenish princess
    - **THEODORIC I** (c. 485-534) King of Reims (511-534)
      - married c. 505 Suavegotta
        - **THEODEBERT I** (c. 505-548) Kings of Reims (534-548)
          - married Wisigarda
            - **THEODEBALD** (535-555) King of Reims (548-555)
  - married (2) in 493 Clotilda (d. 545)
    - **CHLODOMIR** (c. 495-524) King of Orléans (511-524)
    - **CHILDEBERT I** (c. 495-558) King of Paris (511-558)
    - **CHLOTAR I** (c. 497-561) King of Soissons (511-561) King of Reims (555-561) King of the Franks (558-561)
      - married (1) Ingonde
        - **CHARIBERT** (521-567) King of Paris (561-567)
        - **GUNTRAM** (c. 525-592) King of Orléans and Burgundy (561-592)
        - **SIGEBERT I** (535-575) King of Reims and Austrasia (561-575)
          - married c. 566 Brunhild (d. 613)
            - **CHILDEBERT II** (c. 570-c.595) King of Austrasia (575-595) King of Burgundy (592-595)
              - married in 585 Faileube (d. 596)
                - **THEODEBERT II** (585-612) King of Austrasia (595-612)
                - **THEODORIC II** (587-613) King of Burgundy (595-613) King of Austrasia (612-613)
      - married (2) Aregonde (d. 575)
        - **CHILPERIC I** (539 ?-584) King of Soissons and Neustria (561-584)
          - married Fredegunde (d. 597)
            - **CHLOTAR II** (584-629) King of Neustria (584-629) King of the Franks (613-629)
              - married pre-604 Bertrude (d. 620)
                - **DAGOBERT I** (c. 604-639) King of Austrasia (623-639) King of Neustria and Burgundy (629-639) King of the Franks (632-639)
                  - married c. 630 Nantilda
                    - **CLOVIS II** (c. 635-657) King of Neustria and Burgundy (639-657)
                      - married in 651 Bathilda (d. 680)
                        - **CHLOTAR III** (652-673) King of Neustria and Burgundy (657-673)
                        - **CHILDERIC II** (c. 653-675) King of Austrasia (662-675) King of the Franks (673-675)
                          - married Bilichilde
                            - **CHILPERIC II** (c. 670-721) King of Neustria (715-721) King of the Franks (c. 720-721)
                              - **CHILDERIC III** (d. 755) King of the Franks (743-751)
                        - **THEODORIC III** (c. 654-691) King of Neustria and Burgundy in 673 and 675-691 King of the Franks (679-691)
                          - married Clothilda
                            - **CLOVIS IV** (c. 682-695) King of the Franks (691-695)
                            - **CHILDEBERT III** (c. 683-711) King of the Franks (695-711)
                              - **DAGOBERT III** (c. 699-715) King of the Franks (711-715)
                                - **THEODORIC IV** (c. 713-737) King of the Franks (721-737)
                  - married Ragnetrude
                    - **SIGEBERT III** (c. 631-656) King of Austrasia (634-656)
                      - married Immichilde
                        - **DAGOBERT II** (c. 652-679) King of Austrasia (676-679)
                - **CHARIBERT II** (c. 606-632) King of Aquitaine (629-632)

768 : Charlemagne becomes King of the Franks.
772 : Charlemagne launches campaigns against the Saxons (ÿ 803).
778 : Charlemagne launches an expedition in the Iberian Peninsula. Death of Roland at the mountain pass at Roncesvalles.
c. 780 : Introduction of the missi dominici, Charlemagne's envoys in the provinces.
800 : Charlemagne is crowned in Rome as Emperor by Pope Leo III.
814 : Death of Charlemagne.
He is succeeded by his son, Louis I the Pious.
c. 820 : Start of the Viking raids along the French coast then inland.
The main invasion begins in 856 A.D.
840 : Death of Emperor Louis I the Pious. Under the terms of the Treaty of Verdun (843), the Empire is divided between his three sons, Lothair I, Louis the German and Charles II the Bald.
851 : Charles II the Bald recognises Brittany's independence.
858 : Girart of Vienne founds the monastery in Vézelay.
885-886 : The Vikings besiege Paris which is defended by Count Eudes.
1st half of the 10th century: The kingdom is divided into principalities.
910 : Cluny Abbey is founded by William the Pious.
911 : Treaty of Saint-Clair-sur-Epte signed by King Charles III the Simple and Rollo, the Viking chief, who is granted territory.
987 : Death of King Louis V the Lazy. Leading members of the nobility elect Hugh Capet, Duke of the Franks, to the throne of France.

The Carolingians

This dynasty of kings and emperors reigned over part of Western Europe from the middle of the 8th century to the 10th century. It gets its name from its most illustrious member, Charlemagne.

The dynasty's founder was Pepin the Short who, in 751 A.D, put an end to the Merovingian dynasty by deposing Childeric III and having himself proclaimed King of the Franks.

His son, Charlemagne, continued the conquests and unified much of Western Europe before having himself crowned Holy Roman Emperor in 800 A.D. In 843, however, the Empire was divided between Charlemagne's three grandsons and the western area gave rise to the first French territory, Francia occidentalis. It was here that the Carolingian kings succeeded each other for 150 years, from Charles the Bald to Louis V.

Over the 10th century, the Carolingian monarchy fell into a decline. It was incapable of preventing the division of the kingdom of France into principalities and unable to fight foreign invasions. The death of King Louis V the Lazy in 987 A.D. marked the end of the French branch of the Carolingian dynasty. ■

◄ Church in Saint-Germiny-des-Prés (Loiret) dating from the Carolingian period.

Recumbent statue of Carloman (867-884). St. Dennis' Basilica Seine-Saint-Denis.

The Carolingian dynasty

Charlemagne (747-814) King of the Franks (768-814) Emperor of the Western World (800-814)

When he became King of the Franks upon the death of his father, Pepin the Short, in 768 A.D, Charlemagne inherited a kingdom which he then set about extending considerably. He was a soldier and conqueror who spent most of his life warmongering in Italy, the Iberian Peninsula, Bavaria and against the Saxons. In 30 years, he built up a vast Empire covering much of Western Europe. In 800 A.D, Charlemagne had himself crowned Emperor in Rome, by Pope Leo III. Domestic policy during his reign was marked by attempts at organising administrative services (the kingdom was divided into counties, there were regular meetings between leading lay and ecclesiastical dignitaries, capitularies were promulgated and missi dominici were sent out into the provinces). As far as coinage was concerned, he confirmed the royal monopoly on minting money. The sovereign built up a central government, with himself at its heart. The Court settled in Aix-la-Chapelle in 807 A.D. and the town then became the country's capital. Finally, Charlemagne's reign was marked by an intellectual and artistic revival (schools were set up, he attracted educated men such as Alcuin, Eginhard or Paul Diacre to his Court and religious buildings were erected). On his death in 814 A.D, his last surviving son, Louis I, succeeded him at the head of the Empire.

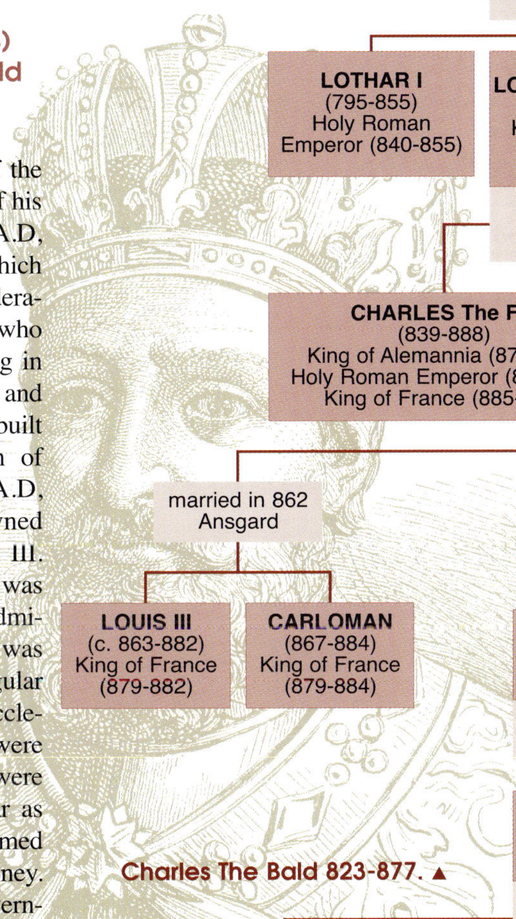

Charles The Bald 823-877. ▲

- **CHARLEMAGNE** (747-814) King of the Franks (768-814) Holy Roman Emperor (800-814)
  - pre-771 married Hildegarde (d. 783)
    - **LOUIS I The Pious** (778-840) Holy Roman Emperor (814-840)
      - married in 798 Ermengard (d. 818)
        - **LOTHAR I** (795-855) Holy Roman Emperor (840-855)
        - **LOUIS The German** (c. 806-876) King of Germany (843-876)
          - married in 827 Emma (d. 876)
            - **CHARLES The Fat** (839-888) King of Alemannia (876-888) Holy Roman Emperor (881-887) King of France (885-887)
      - married in 819 Judith (d. 843)
        - **CHARLES II The Bald** (823-877) King of Western Francia (840-877) Holy Roman Emperor (875-877)
          - married in 842 Ermentrud (d. 869)
            - **LOUIS II The Stammerer** (846-879) King of France (877-879)
              - married in 862 Ansgard
                - **LOUIS III** (c. 863-882) King of France (879-882)
                - **CARLOMAN** (867-884) King of France (879-884)
              - married in 878 Adelaide (d. 901)
                - **CHARLES III The Simple** (879-929) King of France (893-923)
                  - married c. 918 Eadgiva of Wessex
                    - **LOUIS IV From Overseas** (c. 920-954) King of France (936-954)
                      - married in 939 Gerberg (d. 984)
                        - **LOTHAR** (941-986) King of France (954-986)
                          - married in 966 Emma
                            - **LOUIS V The Lazy** (c. 967-987) King of France (986-987)

N.B. The weakening of the Carolingian monarchy from the late 9th century onwards paved the way for the election, by the leading members of the nobility of the kingdom, of kings from the Robertian family i.e. ancestors of the Capetians. This meant that Eudes (888-898), Robert I (922-923) and Rudolph (923-936) became Kings of France.

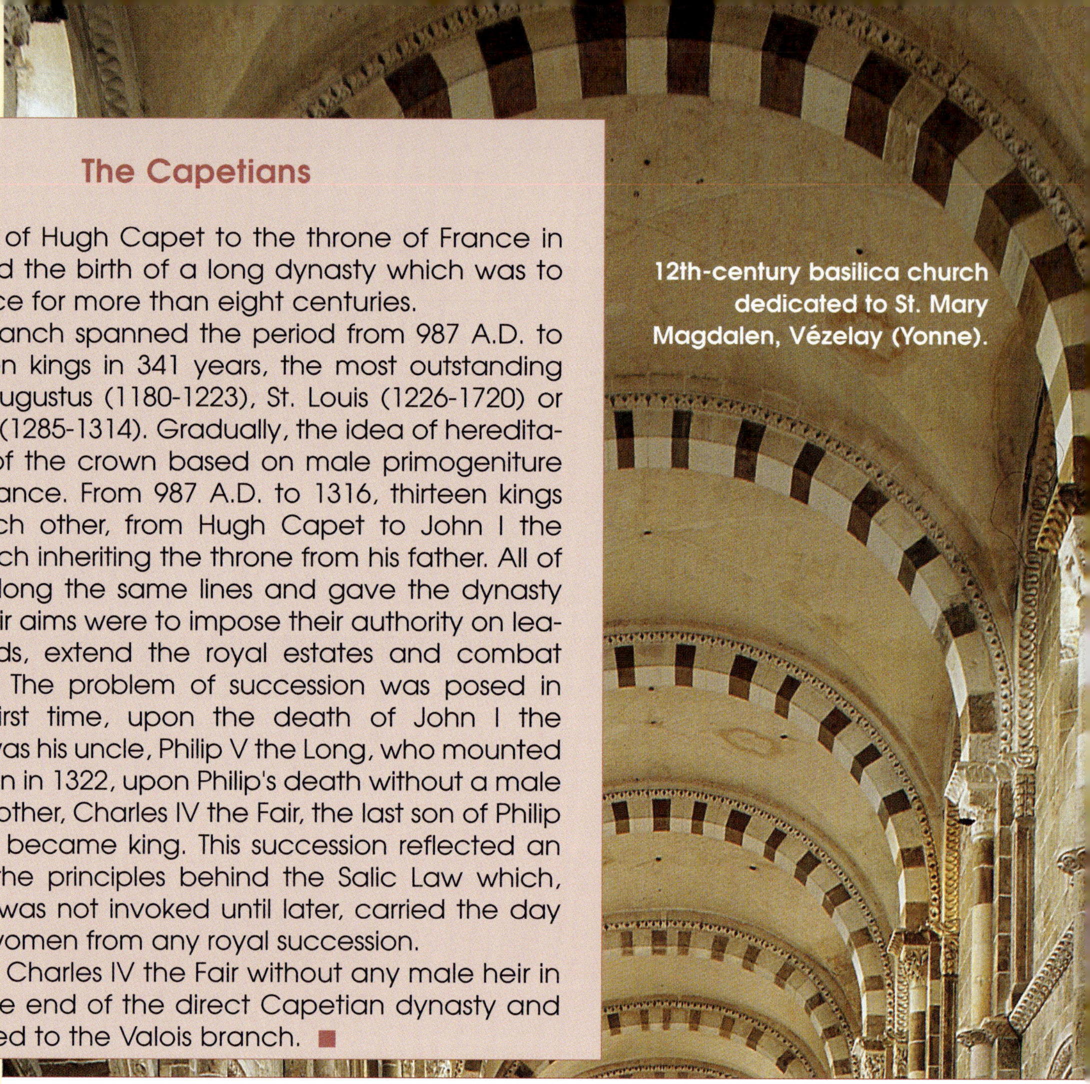

12th-century basilica church dedicated to St. Mary Magdalen, Vézelay (Yonne).

The Capetians

The election of Hugh Capet to the throne of France in 987 A.D. marked the birth of a long dynasty which was to reign over France for more than eight centuries.

The direct branch spanned the period from 987 A.D. to 1328, with fifteen kings in 341 years, the most outstanding being Philip II Augustus (1180-1223), St. Louis (1226-1720) or Philip IV the Fair (1285-1314). Gradually, the idea of hereditary transmission of the crown based on male primogeniture gained acceptance. From 987 A.D. to 1316, thirteen kings succeeded each other, from Hugh Capet to John I the Posthumous, each inheriting the throne from his father. All of them worked along the same lines and gave the dynasty strong roots. Their aims were to impose their authority on leading feudal lords, extend the royal estates and combat foreign powers. The problem of succession was posed in 1316, for the first time, upon the death of John I the Posthumous. It was his uncle, Philip V the Long, who mounted the throne. Again in 1322, upon Philip's death without a male heir, it was his brother, Charles IV the Fair, the last son of Philip IV the Fair, who became king. This succession reflected an application of the principles behind the Salic Law which, even though it was not invoked until later, carried the day and excluded women from any royal succession.

The death of Charles IV the Fair without any male heir in 1328 marked the end of the direct Capetian dynasty and the crown passed to the Valois branch. ■

Late 10th century mid 11th century :	The bishops hold a number of councils in an effort to impose the "Peace of God" on noblemen.
c. 1020-1050 :	The principle of vassaldom and the links between vassals and liege lords are more clearly defined.
c. 1024-1089 :	Mont Saint-Michel Abbey is built.
post-1050 :	Romanesque architecture reaches its heyday.
c. 1077-1082 :	The Bayeux Tapestry is stitched.
1095 :	Pope Urban II preaches the first Crusade to the Holy Land at the Council of Clermont.
12th century :	Numerous towns obtain borough charters and are freed from the control of local lords.
1109-1119 :	Conflict between Louis VI the Fat and King Henry I of England over ownership of Normandy (also in 1123-1124).
c. 1118 :	The Order of the Temple is founded in Jerusalem by French knights.
c. 1132 :	Work begins on the building of the basilica in Saint-Denis. Gothic architecture is introduced and developed.
1137 :	Marriage of the Crown Prince, Louis, with Eleanor of Aquitaine.
1147-1149 :	King Louis VII takes part in the Second Crusade to the Holy Land.
post 1150-1160 :	Catharism spreads and becomes a veritable religious faith.
1152 :	King Louis VII and Eleanor of Aquitaine are divorced. Eleanor remarries, with Henry of England.
1180 :	Philip II Augustus becomes king.
1184 :	Start of tours by bailiffs, the king's local representatives.
1190 :	Work begins on the construction of the Louvre in Paris.
1190-1191 :	Philip II Augustus takes part in the Third Crusade.
1194-1199 :	War between Philip II Augustus and Richard the Lionheart, King of England.

1202-1214 : Renewed warfare between King Philip II Augustus and King John of England. The King of France is victorious at Bouvines in 1214.
1209-1226 : Crusades against the Albigensians (Cathars).
1226 : Accession of Louis IX (St. Louis).
1233 : The Inquisition arrives in Languedoc.
1244 : Surrender of the Cathar fortress in Montségur.
1248-1254 : Seventh Crusade in the Holy Land. King Louis IX takes part in battles in Egypt and Syria.
1250-1270 : Numerous hilltop towns ("bastides") are built in Aquitaine.
c. 1250 : End of major land clearances in country areas.
c. 1257 : Robert de Sorbon founds a college in Paris, the "Sorbonne".
1270 : Louis IX takes part in the Eighth Crusade and dies in Tunis.
1285 : Philip IV the Fair becomes king.
1294-1299 : Conflict between Philip IV the Fair and King Edward I of England.
post-1300 : Decline of the fairs in Champagne which had been major events, famous throughout the Western world in the 13th century.
1302 : Revolt in Flanders against French occupation. King Philip IV the Fair wins the Battle of Mons-en-Pévèle in 1304.
1307 : King Philip IV the Fair has the Knights Templar arrested. They are executed in 1310. Their Grand Master, Jacques de Molay, is put to death in 1314.
1309 : Start of the Avignon papacy with Pope Clement V.
1315 : Implementation of the salt tax.
1316 : Philip V the Long, brother of the deceased King Louis, mounts the throne.
1317 : An assembly of leading noblemen adopts the principle preventing women from mounting the throne of France.
1328 : Death of King Charles IV the Fair. End of the direct Capetian branch.
c. 1328 : Census of parishes and homes in the kingdom.

Philip II Augustus (1165-1223) – King of France (1180-1223)

Philip II Augustus became king at the age of fifteen and spent much of his reign warmongering, successfully and extensively increasing the royal estates. His victory over a coalition of leading noblemen from Flanders, Champagne and Burgundy gave him control of Artois, Vermandois and Amiens (1185). However, the main focus of his reign was the struggle against England, firstly against Richard the Lionheart (1194-1199) then against King John (1202-1217). Philip Augustus took Normandy, Touraine, Anjou and the Poitiers area. The main event in the war was the French victory over a foreign coalition at the Battle of Bouvines (1214). His reign was also marked by a strengthening of central control through the appointment of bailiffs or seneschals. The crusade against the Cathars, which began in 1209, gave the monarchy a foothold in the South of France. Philip Augustus was also involved in a serious conflict with the papacy because of his successive marriages (1196-1200). Finally, it was during his reign that Paris became the capital of the kingdom. The king then commissioned the building of town walls and the first Louvre Palace.

Bayeux tapestry (11th century). Musée Guillaume le Conquérant (Calvados).

The direct Capetian dynasty

A 19th-century stained-glass window depicting St. Louis. Cathedral of Notre-Dame-la Grande, Poitiers (Vienne). ▲

Louis IX or St. Louis (1214-1270)
King of France (1226-1270)

Louis IX became king at the age of twelve and his mother, Blanche of Castile, remained Regent until 1234. Under the terms of the Treaty of Meaux, she ended the Albigensian Crusade (1229) and prepared the annexation of the County of Toulouse to the crown of France. The hostilities between France and England re-opened in 1242 but the King of France sought a lasting, fair peace. He signed the Treaty of Paris with Henry III in 1258; this led to reciprocal territorial concessions. Louis IX's domestic policies were marked by a desire for order and justice. During his reign, France enjoyed great moral, intellectual and artistic influence throughout Europe. Louis IX was a fervently devout sovereign and as such he took part in the last two crusades to the Holy Land (1248-1254 and 1270). It was during the last crusade that he died of plague during an epidemic that swept through the crusader army under the walls of Tunis. Louis was canonised in 1297.

HUGH I CAPET
(c. 941-996)
King of France
(987-996)

m. pre-970
Adelaide
(c.945-c.1004)
daughter of the
Count of Poitiers

ROBERT II The Pious
(c. 972-1031)
King of France
(996-1031)

m. c. 1003
Constance of Arles
(c. 983-1032)
daughter of Count
William I

HENRI I
(1008-1060)
King of France (1031-1060)

m. 1051
Anne
(c.1024-post 1075) daughter of the
Grand Duke of Kiev

PHILIP I
(c. 1052-1108)
King of France (1060-1108)

m. 1071
Bertha of Holland
(c.1055-1094)
(repudiated in 1091)

LOUIS VI The Fat
(c.1081-1137)
King of France
(1108-1137)

m. 1115
Adelaide of Savoy
(c.1100-1154)

m. 1137
Eleanor of
Aquitaine
(1122-1204)
(annulment in 1152)

LOUIS VII The Younger
(1120-1180)
King of France
(1137-1180)

m. 1160
Adela of
Champagne
(c.1140-1206)

PHILIP II AUGUSTUS
(1165-1223)
King of France (1180-1223)

m. 1180
Isabella (1170-1190)
daughter of the Count of Hainaut

LOUIS VIII The Lion
(1187-1226)
King of France (1223-1226)

m. 1200
Blanche (1188-1252)
daughter of the King of Castile

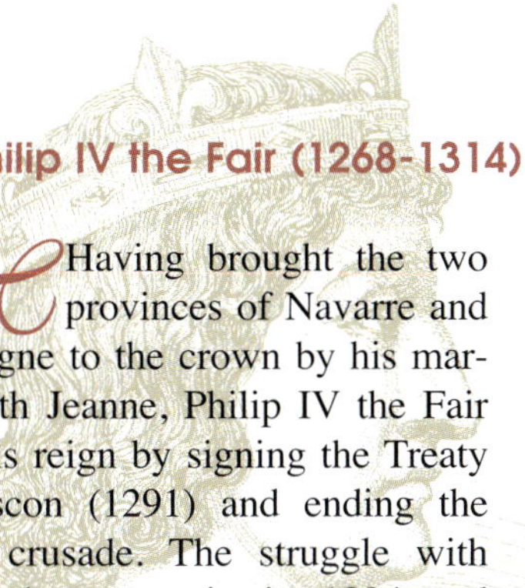

Philip IV the Fair (1268-1314) King of France (1285-1314)

Having brought the two provinces of Navarre and Champagne to the crown by his marriage with Jeanne, Philip IV the Fair began his reign by signing the Treaty of Tarascon (1291) and ending the Aragon crusade. The struggle with England began again in 1294 and ended with the Treaty of Montreuil (1299). Under the terms of the Treaty of Paris (1303), Philip the Fair handed the conquered territories back to Edward I. The alliance between England and Flanders led to the region's occupation by the French in 1300. They were chased out of Bruges then defeated at Courtrai (1302) but took their revenge at the Battle of Mons-en-Pévèle (1304). The King of France was then able to annex Flanders. The numerous wars depleted the kingdom's coffers and Philip the Fair was forced to devalue French currency several times between 1290 and 1309. He confiscated the property of Lombards and Jews in 1292 but, more importantly, his determination to impose exceptional taxes on the clergy brought him into serious conflict with the Pope from 1296 onwards. The king convened a meeting of the three Orders of the kingdom (1302) in a forerunner of the future States General; the Orders provided him with their support. Financial difficulties led Philip the Fair into conflict with the Order of the Knights Templar. The Order was closed down and its members executed (1307-1314). As to the monarch's domestic policies, they were aimed at a strengthening of royal prerogatives and in this he was assisted by his legal advisers (Pierre Flot, Enguerran de Marigny, Guillaume de Nogaret). His policy led him to convene frequent meetings of the three Orders to seek approval for his ideas.

Philip IV The Fair (1268-1314). ▲

The Conciergerie. Philip the Fair redesigned and extended the entire palace on the Ile de la Cité in Paris. ▶▲

The Sainte-Chapelle in Paris was consecrated in 1248.
consacrée en 1248, Paris. ▼

LOUIS IX (St. Louis)
(1214-1270)
King of France (1226-1270)
m. 1234
Margaret (1221-1295)
daughter of the Count of Provence

PHILIP III The Bold
(1245-1285)
King of France
(1270-1285)
m. 1262 Isabella
(1234-1271)
daughter of the King of Aragon

Robert
(1256-1317)
Count of Clermont

8th-generation Bourbon dynasty

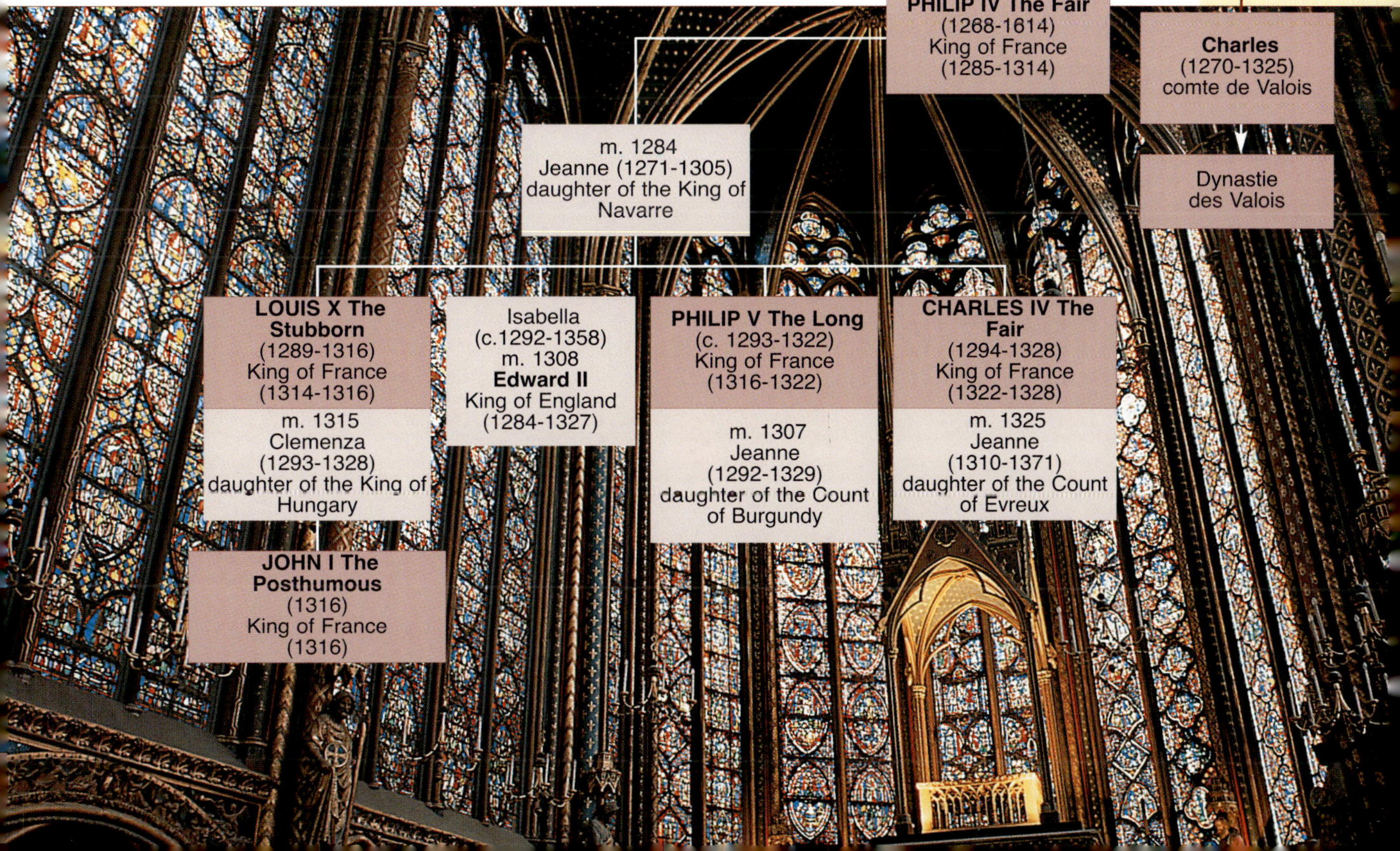

PHILIP IV The Fair
(1268-1614)
King of France
(1285-1314)

Charles
(1270-1325)
comte de Valois

Dynastie des Valois

m. 1284
Jeanne (1271-1305)
daughter of the King of Navarre

LOUIS X The Stubborn
(1289-1316)
King of France
(1314-1316)
m. 1315
Clemenza
(1293-1328)
daughter of the King of Hungary

JOHN I The Posthumous
(1316)
King of France
(1316)

Isabella
(c.1292-1358)
m. 1308
Edward II
King of England
(1284-1327)

PHILIP V The Long
(c. 1293-1322)
King of France
(1316-1322)
m. 1307
Jeanne
(1292-1329)
daughter of the Count of Burgundy

CHARLES IV The Fair
(1294-1328)
King of France
(1322-1328)
m. 1325
Jeanne
(1310-1371)
daughter of the Count of Evreux

In 1369, Charles V commissioned the completion of the keep in Vincennes (Val-de-Marne) on which building work had commenced in 1361, during the reign of his father. ▲

The direct Valois line

1337 : King Philip VI confiscates the Duchy of Guyenne from the King of England. Start of the Hundred Years' War.

1346 : The French army is routed by the English at Crécy.

1348-1349 : Major plague epidemic throughout the kingdom.

1356 : King John II the Good of France is captured by the English at the Battle of Poitiers. The States General try to impose the introduction of a parliamentary monarchy on Charles, the heir to the throne, in 1357.

1358 : A revolt led by Etienne Marcel, Provost of Merchants, is put down in Paris. A peasant uprising, the "Jacquerie", breaks out in the Beauvais area.

1360 : King John II the Good is released.

1364 : Du Guesclin wins the Battle of Cocherel, defeating King Charles V the Bad of Navarre.

1372-1373 : King Charles V and Du Guesclin take control of most of the English possessions – Limousin, Poitou, Aunis and Saintonge.

1392 : King Charles VI becomes insane.

1407 : Start of the civil war between Armagnacs and Burgundians.

1415 : The French army is defeated by the English at Azincourt.

1420 : Signature of the Treaty of Troyes by King Charles VI and King Henry V of England. The heir to the French throne, Charles, is disinherited.

1429-1431 : Joan of Arc intervenes in the Hundred Years' War.

1438 : King Charles VII pronounces the Pragmatic Sanction of Bourges, the first expression of Gallicanism.

1439 : Direct taxation becomes permanent in order to main tain an army.

The direct Valois line

This branch of the Capetian dynasty acceded to the throne of France in 1328 with Philip VI, son of Charles de Valois and nephew of Philip IV the Fair whose three sons had died without leaving a male heir. The new king was chosen by the leading dignitaries of the kingdom in preference to King Edward III of England despite the fact that Edward was Philip IV the Fair's grandson through his mother, Isabel.

The Valois dynasty reigned over France from 1328 to 1589 and produced three lines. The direct Valois line gave seven kings to France from 1328 to 1498, from Philip VI to Charles VIII. During this 170-year period, the throne again passed from father to son. These were difficult times, marked by the Hundred Years' War, the imprisonment of King John the Good, the madness of Charles VI and the civil war between Armagnacs and Burgundians. The second half of the 15th century saw a return of royal authority with the kings Charles VII (1422-1461) and Louis XI (1461-1483).

In 1498, Charles VIII died without leaving a male heir and the crown passed to the nearest living prince of the blood, his cousin the Duke of Orléans, who became King Louis XII. ■

Louis XI (1423-1483) – King of France (1461-1483)

Louis XI, eldest son of Charles VII, spent his father's reign plotting against him (in 1440 during the Praguerie Revolt then again in 1456). In 1447, Louis received the governorship of Dauphiné. When he finally mounted the throne on the death of his father in 1461, he was able to build on the order given to the kingdom, an order which he maintained in financial and legal areas. By doing so, he was able to continue the territorial construction of France by fighting the last great feudal noblemen, in particular the Duke of Burgundy. In 1465, Louis XI was faced with a revolt by princes who had joined forces in the League of the Public Weal. Another feudal revolt, under the leadership of Charles the Bold, Duke of Burgundy, led to the Meeting in Péronne at which the King of France was held prisoner by Charles and was released only under humiliating conditions (1468).

Thereafter, Charles the Bold was the kingdom's main enemy and his power had to be reduced. The struggle lasted until 1477. Louis XI gradually isolated him by giving his own brother, Charles, the Duchy of Guyenne in 1469 then by signing the Treaty of Picquigny with Edward IV of England in 1475. Charles the Bold's claims led to revolt by the Swiss and Alsatians. He was defeated at Grandson and Morat (1476) and killed at the Siege of Nancy in 1477. Burgundy and Picardy were then annexed to the crown.

Louis XI acquired further land in 1480-1481, namely Anjou, Maine and Provence. He stimulated economic growth by tax exemptions, improvements to the transport system and encouragement for the setting up of fairs. His sole surviving son, Charles, succeeded him in 1483.

◄ Louis XI, 1423-1483.

The direct Valois line

- **. c 1440-1470 :** Start of rural reconstruction and a gradual return to prosperity.
- **1453 :** French victory at Castillon-la-Bataille. End of the Hundred Years' War. The English have only one possession left in France, Calais.
- **1461 :** Accession of King Louis XI.
- **1477 :** Death of Charles the Bold, Duke of Burgundy, at the Battle of Nancy. Louis XI occupies Burgundy, Picardy and the Artois area.
- **1480-1481 :** The counties of Anjou, Maine and Provence are annexed to the crown.
- **1491 :** King Charles VIII marries Anne of Brittany.
- **1494 :** Start of the Italian Campaign. French armies wage war in the peninsula.

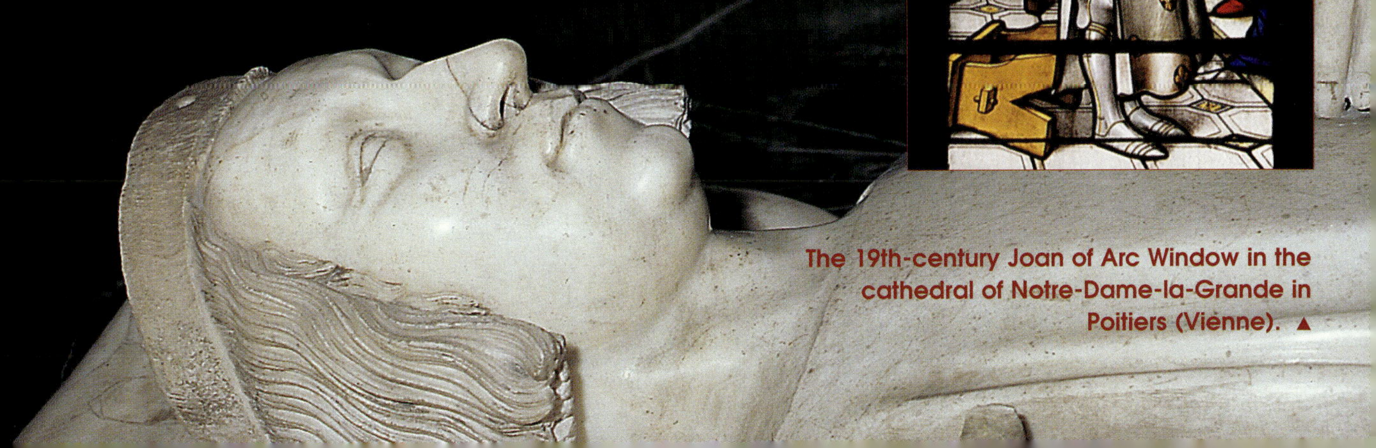

Recumbent statue of Charles V The Wise (1338-1380). St. Dennis' Basilica (Seine-Saint-Denis). ▼

The 19th-century Joan of Arc Window in the cathedral of Notre-Dame-la-Grande in Poitiers (Viénne). ▲

The direct Valois line

Charles VIII, 1470-1498. ▲

14th-century Chamber of the Gentlemen-at-Arms, Conciergerie, Paris. ▼

PHILIP VI de Valois
(1293-1350)
King of France
(1328-1350)

m. 1313
Jeanne
(1294-1348)
daughter of the Duke of Burgundy

JOHN II The Good
(1319-1364)
King of France
(1350-1364)

m. 1332
Bonne
(1315-1349)
daughter of the King of Bohemia

CHARLES V The Wise
(1338-1380)
King of France
(1364-1380)

m. 1350
Jeanne
(1338-1377)
daughter of the Duc de Bourbon

LOUIS, Duc d'Orléans
(1372-1407)

m. 1389
Valentine Visconti
(1366-1408)

Valois-Orléans dynasty

CHARLES VI The Mad
(1368-1422)
King of France
(1380-1422)

m. 1385
Isabella
(1369-1435)
daughter of the Duke of Bavaria

CHARLES VII The Victorious
(1403-1461)
King of France
(1422-1461)

m. 1422
Mary
(1404-1463)
daughter of the King of Naples

LOUIS XI
(1423-1483)
King of France
(1461-1483)

m. 1451
Charlotte
(1443-1483)
daughter of the Duke of Savoy

CHARLES VIII
(1470-1498)
King of France
(1483-1498)

m. 1491
Anne
(1476-1514)
daughter of the Duke of Brittany

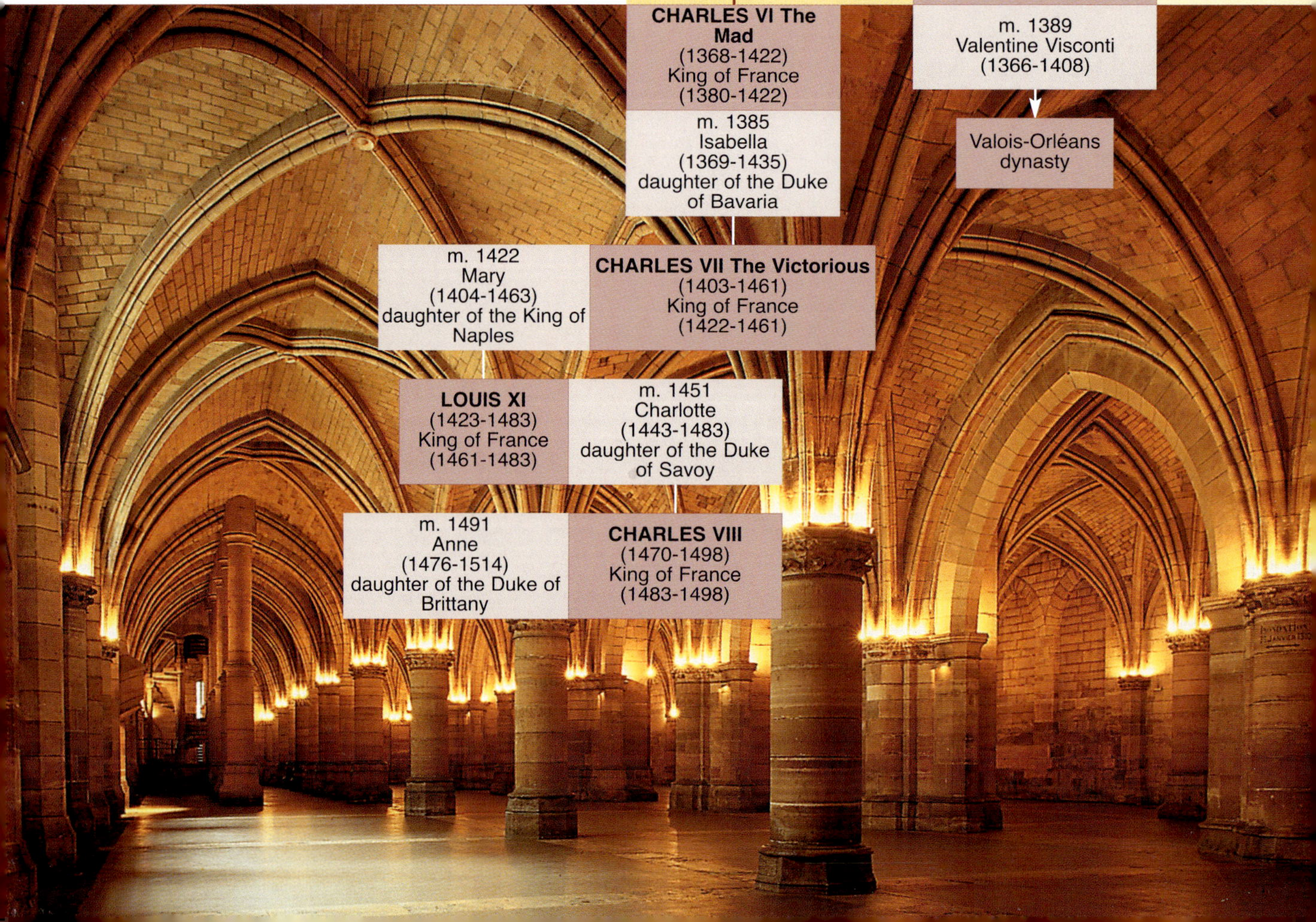

Modern France

Loggia façade (c. 1520), Blois Castle (Loir-et-Cher). ▸

The Valois-Orléans and Valois-Angoulême lines

The Valois-Orléans line (1498-1515) produced only one king in the person of Louis XII. This branch descended from Duke Louis d'Orléans, brother of King Charles VI the Insane.

Louis XII died without a male heir in 1515 and the crown passed to his son-in-law, François I, who was also descended from Duke Louis d'Orléans through his father, Charles d'Angoulême. The Valois-Angoulême line reigned over France from 1515 to 1589 and gave the country five kings, from François I to Henri III. After the reigns of François I (1515-1547) and his son, Henri II (1547-1559), which marked the "fine 16th century", the monarchy lost power and was faced with the Wars of Religion. Henri II's three sons succeeded each other on the throne of France but were incapable of putting a stop to the civil war. Moreover, they all died without a male heir.

In 1589, the death of Henri III gave the crown to the King of Navarre, Henri, the nearest heir to the throne, who founded the Bourbon dynasty. ■

François I (1494-1547) – King of France (1515-1547)

François I was the archetypal Renaissance knight. As soon as he mounted the throne, he relaunched the Italian campaign, winning victory at the Battle of Marignano. The main focus of François I's reign was his long-standing rivalry with Emperor Charles V. An initial war (1521) caused the French to abandon the Milan area. In 1525, François I was defeated and captured at Pavia. He was taken to Spain as a prisoner and was not released until he had signed the disastrous Treaty of Madrid (1526) which he then refused to uphold. Despite a further expedition into Italy led by the French monarch, peace was signed in 1529. War began again in 1535 but to no avail and a truce was signed in 1538. One final confrontation took place from 1542 onwards and the French were victorious at the Battle of Cerisole (1544) but, under the terms of the Treaty of Crépy-en-Laonnais, François I waived his claims to the Artois area and Flanders and left the Milan region to his adversary.

On the domestic front, François I's reign was marked by one major change – the introduction of the absolute monarchy. From then on, the king's authority was no longer called into question and the nobility became courtiers, receiving income from the sovereign. François I continued the administrative unification of the kingdom through the Order of Villers-Cotterêts (1539). In the area of religion, Protestantism, which had long been tolerated by the king, began to be persecuted after the "Placards Affair" (1534). During François I's reign, life at court developed and symbolised the luxury of the Renaissance. Arts and letters enjoyed the monarch's patronage and the arrival of Leonardo da Vinci brought the Italian Renaissance to France. François I commissioned numerous castles and palaces (Chambord, Fontainebleau, Saint-Germain-en-Laye) and began the reconstruction of the Louvre.

East façade of the 16th-century Château de Fontainebleau (Seine-et-Marne). ▲

Late 15th-mid 16th century : Construction of the Loire Valley castles and palaces.

1498 : Death of King Charles VIII. Accession of his cousin, Louis XII, Duke of Orléans. In 1499, he married Anne of Brittany.

1499 : King Louis XII launches a further Italian Campaign.
France waives its claims to the Milan area in 1513.

1515 : Accession of François I. The Italian Campaign is again launched with a view to taking over the Milan area. François I is victorious at Marignano and occupies Milan. Leonardo da Vinci sett les in France.

1516 : Concordat of Bologna between King François I and Pope Leo X.

1520 : The Field of the Cloth of Gold, a meeting between François I and Henry VIII of England.

1521 : War between François I and Charles V, the German Emperor.

1522 : King François I gives an official framework to the system of payment for office.

1524 : Death of Bayard at the Battle of Sesia in Italy.

1525 : The French are defeated by the imperial army at Pavia. François is taken prisoner.

1526 : The Treaty of Madrid is signed by François I and Charles V. François I is released.

1527 : The "Ladies Peace" is signed. François I waives his claims to Italy, Flanders and the Artois area; Charles V waives his claims to Burgundy.

1530 : The Royal College is set up by François I. It is the forerunner of the Collège de France.

1532 : Brittany is permanently annexed to France.

1533 : Theologian John Calvin gives his support to the Reformed Religion.

1534 : The "Placards Affair", during which Lutheran pamphlets are displayed in several towns in which the Court resides. Jacques Cartier arrives in Canada.

1539 : Order of Villers-Cotterêts.

1546 : King François I commissions architect Pierre Lescot to build a new Louvre Palace in Paris.

1515, Battle of Marignano. ▶

The Valois-Orléans and Valois-Angoulême lines

François I (1494-1547). ▸

LOUIS XII
(1462-1515)
grandson of Louis, Duc d'Orléans
King of France (1498-1515)

m. 1499
Anne of Brittany
(1476-1514)
widow of King Charles VIII of France

Claude
(1499-1524)

m. 1514

FRANÇOIS I
(1494-1547)
King of France
(1515-1547)

HENRI II
(1519-1559)
King of France
(1547-1559)

m. 1533
Catherine de Medici
(1519-1589)

FRANÇOIS II
(1544-1560)
King of France
(1559-1560)

CHARLES IX
(1550-1574)
King of France
(1560-1574)

HENRI III
(1551-1589)
King of France
(1574-1589)

Marguerite
(1553-1615)
("Queen Margot")

m. 1572

HENRI IV
(1553-1610)
King of Navarre (1572-1610)
King of France (1589-1610)
(marriage annulled in 1599)

1547 : A special court (the "chambre ardente") is set up in the Parliament to repress the Lutheran heresy.
1552 : War begins again between Henri II, King of France, and the German Emperor, Charles V.
1559 : The Treaty of Cateau-Cambrésis is signed by France, England and Spain. End of the Italian Campaign.
1560 : Accession of Charles IX. His mother, Catherine de Medici, becomes Regent.
1562 : Start of the Wars of Religion.
1572 : St. Bartholomew's Day Massacre of the country's Protestants.
1574 : Death of King Charles IX. Accession of his brother, Henri III.
c. 1575-1595 : General economic slump in industry, commerce, ban king and society at large.
1579 : Grand Edict of Blois covering various aspects of society.
1589 : King Henri III is assassinated by a monk named Jacques Clément. Henri of Navarre becomes King of France under the title Henri IV.

Henri II, 1519-1559. ▸

The Bourbons

The Bourbon kings represented a branch of the Capetian dynasty. The first Bourbon, Henri IV, King of Navarre, mounted the throne of France in 1589. The Bourbons were descended from Henri's father, Antoine de Bourbon, an eighth-generation descendent of Robert, St. Louis' son.

The Bourbons reigned from 1589 to 1792 and again from 1814 to 1830, giving France seven kings. Louis XIII and Louis XIV implemented a system of absolute monarchy which was swept away by the French Revolution in 1789 during which Louis XVI was overthrown and executed.

However, the dynasty survived through the brothers of the deceased king and, during the Restoration in 1814 (after the interlude of the Revolution and Napoleonic Empire), Louis XVIII and Charles X reigned in their turn.

Afte the 1830 Revolution and the abdication of Charles X, the crown passed to the Orléans line. The French line of the Bourbons ceased to exist in 1883 on the death of the Count of Chambord, the grandson of the last monarch, Charles X. ■

Henri IV, 1553-1610. ▼

1593 : King Henri IV abjures the Protestant faith. He is crowned in 1594 and enters Paris.

1595 : King Henri IV declares war on Spain. The conflict ends with the Treaty of Vervins (1598).

1598 : King Henri IV promulgates the Edict of Nantes which recognises freedom of conscience and puts an end to the Wars of Religion.

early 17th century : Economic recovery and a return to prosperity.

1604 : A royal edict instituting a tax known as the "paulette".

1610 : Henri IV is assassinated by Ravaillac. Accession of his son, Louis XIII. Louis' mother, Marie de Medici, becomes regent.

1624 : Richelieu becomes Louis' principal minister.

1625 : The struggle against the Protestants begins again. The town of La Rochelle is besieged in 1627-1628.

1635 : King Louis XIII creates the Académie Française.
War is declared on Spain. The French become involved in the Thirty Years' War. Start of the wars against the Hapsburgs.
Start of the French conquest of Guadeloupe and Martinique.

1641 : Royal edict limiting the Parliament's powers.

1642 : Death of Richelieu. Cardinal Mazarin becomes principal minister.
The French found Montreal in Canada.

1643 : Accession of Louis XIV. His mother, Anne of Austria, is regent and Mazarin becomes Leader of the Counsel. The French defeat the Spaniards at the Battle of Rocroi.

1648 : Treaties of Westphalia ending the Thirty Years' War.

1648-1653 : Parliamentary uprising then aristocratic uprising against Mazarin.

1661 : Death of Mazarin. Beginning of Louis XIV's personal reign.
Arrest of Fouquet, Superintendent of Finances.

1665 : Colbert is appointed Controller General of Finance.

1667-1668 : War of Devolution against the Spaniards. The town of Lille is taken by the French.

1672-1678 : Dutch War which degenerates into an anti-French coalition.
Louis XIV conquers Franche-Comté and the Artois area.

1678 : Vauban is appointed Commissioner General of Fortifications.

1681 : Louis XIV annexes Strasburg.

1682 : King Louis XIV and the Court move to Versailles.

1685 : The Edict of Nantes is revoked by the Edict of Fontainebleau. Protestant worship is abolished in France.

1688-1697 : War of the League of Augsburg. A second anti-French coalition comes into being.

1693-1694 : Poor harvest, famine, serious economic crisis, widespread poverty.

1701-1714 : War of the Spanish Succession. The French are defeated on several occasions and the country is invaded in 1708.
France is saved by a victory at the Battle of Denain in 1712.

1709 : Major famine, hard winter, economic crisis, widespread poverty, uprisings.

1715 : Louis XV becomes king with Philippe d'Orléans as regent. Government reform.

1720 : Collapse of Law's financial system.

c. 1725 : Freemasonry is introduced into France.

1726 : Fleury becomes Prime Minister.

1733-1738 : War of Polish Succession against the German Empire.
King Stanislaw Leszczynski waives his claim to the throne and is granted Lorraine.

1741-1748 : War of Austrian Succession against England and Austria.

1756-1763 : Seven Years' War against England and Prussia. Fighting in Europe and the colonies in America.
France assigns most of its American possessions.

1768 : France purchases Corsica from the Republic of Genoa.

1777 : Necker is appointed Controller General of Finance by Louis XVI.
La Fayette fights in the USA with the American rebels. The French are involved in the American War of Independence (1780-1783).

1786 : Failure of Calonne's fiscal reform in the face of the worsening financial situation.

1788 : The Parliaments revolt against the fiscal reform drafted by Loménie de Brienne. Louis XVI convenes the States General for May 1789.

The Bourbon dynasty

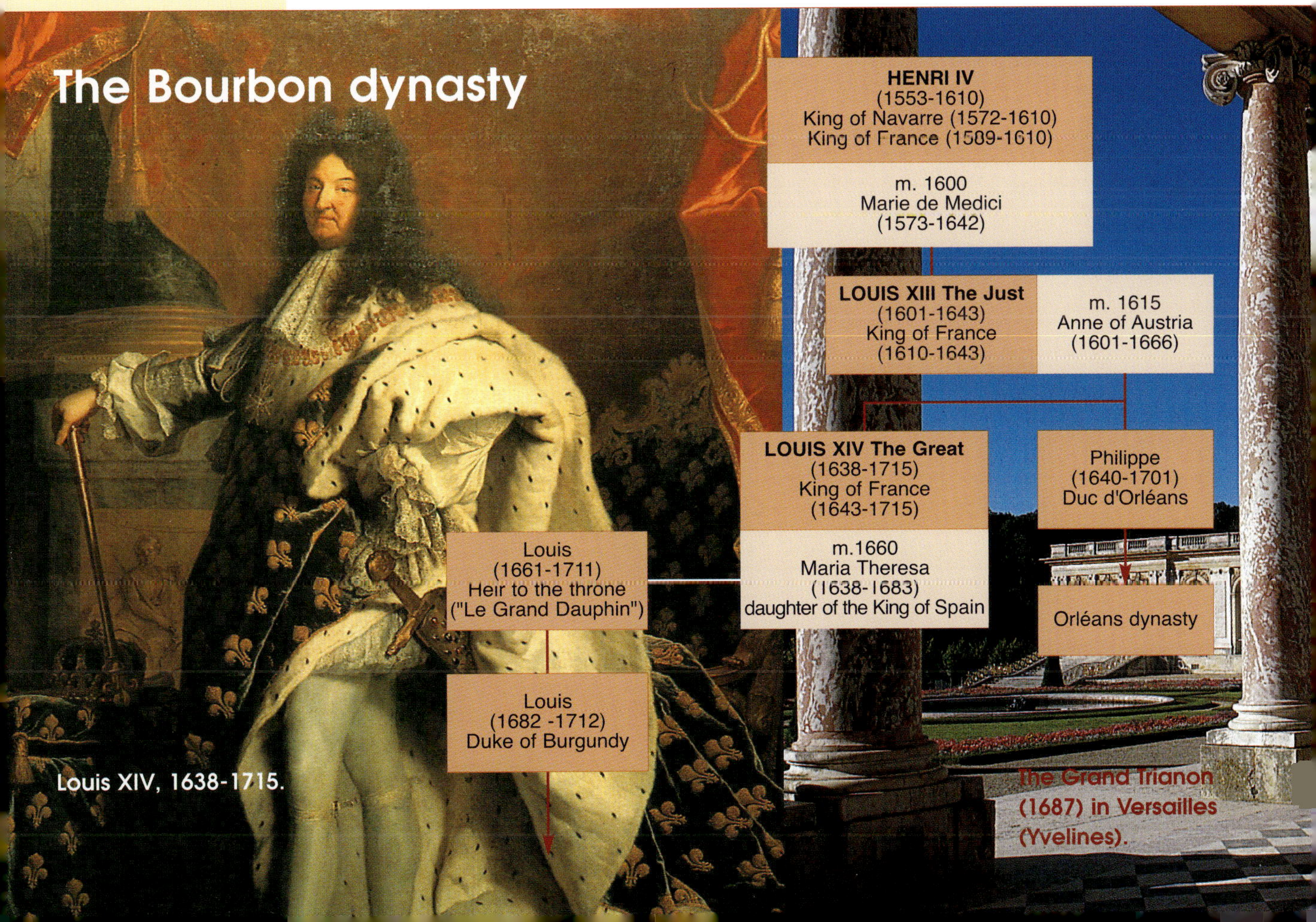

Louis XIV, 1638-1715.

The Grand Trianon (1687) in Versailles (Yvelines).

The Bourbon dynasty (continued)

LOUIS XV The Well-Beloved
(1710-1774)
King of France
(1715-1774)

m. 1725
Marie Leszczynska
(1703-1768)
daughter of the King of Poland

Louis de France
(1729-1765)

LOUIS XVI
(1754-1793)
King of France
(1774-1792)

m. 1770
Marie-Antoinette
(1755-1793)
daughter of the German Emperor

Louis (XVII)
1785-1795

LOUIS XVIII
(1755-1824)
King of France
(1814-1815 and 1815-1824)

m. 1771
Marie-Josèphe of Savoy
(1753-1810)

CHARLES X
(1757-1836)
King of France
(1824-1830)

m. 1773
Marie-Thérèse
(1756-1805)
daughter of the King of Sardinia

Louis XV, 1710-1774. ▲

Louis XVIII, 1755-1824. ▲

Henri IV (1553-1610)
King of Navarre (1572-1610), King of France (1589-1610)

Henri became King of Navarre in 1572 and, that same year, married Marguerite de Valois, the sister of King Charles IX, as a sign of the reconciliation between Roman Catholics and Protestants. Six days later, he survived the St. Bartholomew's Day Massacre by being forcibly converted to Catholicism. In 1576, Henri of Navarre fled the Court, abjured Catholicism and took over the leadership of the Protestant army. He fought the Catholics for several years. On the death of Henri II's last son (1584), he became heir presumptive to the throne of France. After Henri III's assassination in 1589, Henri IV became King of France. His first task was to conquer his kingdom. To do so, he had to fight the Leaguers and their ally, Philip II of Spain. In order to gain acceptance by all the people of France, he eventually abjured his Protestant faith (1593) and had himself crowned in Chartres (1594). This enabled him to make his official entry into Paris. However, he had to continue the fight against the last Leaguers, forcing them into submission, and against Philip II of Spain. Henri IV defeated his enemies at Fontaine-Française (1595) but fighting continued in the north of France until 1598. The two monarchs then signed the Treaty of Vervins, re-establishing peace between France and Spain. That same year, Henri IV achieved religious peace in the country by promulgating the Edict of Nantes. This marked the beginning of a period of restoration of royal authority. The king showed his power by refusing to convene the States General, restricting the claims of Parliaments, and firmly putting down any attempt at revolt by the nobility. In order to ensure the loyalty of his officials, he promulgated an edict introducing the "paulette", a tax making official positions hereditary in return for an annual payment (1604). The work to redress France also concerned the country's economy and finances, and led to the implementation of the policies of Minister Sully. Finally, Henri IV patronised the conquest of Canada where Champlain founded the town of Quebec (1608). In foreign policy, the second part of the reign was marked only by a short war against the Duke of Savoy (1600) from which France emerged victorious. The war brought France the areas of Bresse, Bugey, Valromey and Gex. In 1610, Henri IV was murdered by a fanatic named Ravaillac.

Louis XIV the Great (1638-1715) – King of France (1643-1715)

When Louis XIV succeeded Louis XIII in 1643, he was only five years old and his mother, Anne of Austria, acted as regent until 1651 although it was actually Mazarin who governed until 1661. He put an end to the war against the German Empire by the Treaties of Westphalia (1648). His authoritarian policies led to opposition in 1648, a revolt known as the "Fronde" which was the last brutal manifestation of armed protest against royal authority. The Fronde began as a revolt on the part of parliamentarians in Paris but, in 1650, became a revolt by princes. The Cardinal won the day (1653) but the crisis led to war with Spain. It ended with the signature of the Treaty of the Pyrenees (1659) under which France obtained the Roussillon, Cerdagne and Artois areas as well as many towns in Flanders. On Mazarin's death, Louis XIV inherited a peaceful country whose finances had been redressed. Royal power had also been strengthened. He then began a personal reign that was to last 54 years and leave its mark on the history of France.

Louis XIV announced that he intended to govern on his own. He removed Fouquet from office and nominated ministers who merely executed his orders. The nobility lost any semblance of power and was excluded from politics, especially after the Court moved to Versailles (1682). The role of Parliaments was restricted, the States General were never convened and administrative centralisation was further strengthened through the appointment of Intendents. Then came the concept of royal majesty, of the "Sun King", based on theories of monarchy by divine right. Thanks to major economic development and increased wealth in the country as a whole, not to mention the largest army in Europe, Louis XIV launched an aggressive foreign policy which led to four wars. The War of Devolution (1667-1668) against Spain led to the conquest of fortresses in Flanders, including Lille. The Dutch War (1672-1678), marked by the invasion of the Low Countries, degenerated into a coalition against France but, through the Peace of Nijmegen, brought the country Franche-Comté and the Artois area. The policy of "reunions" instigated by Louis XIV during periods of peace (Strasburg, 1681) led to the War of the League of Augsburg (1688-1697) in which France had difficulty overcoming the enemy. During the final conflict, the War of the Spanish Succession (1701-1714), France suffered major defeats. The victory at the Battle of Denain (1712) gave the country one last chance to lift up its head again and an opportunity to negotiate a peaceful settlement. France came out of these numerous wars in ruins and impoverished. In religious areas, Louis XIV behaved like the head of the Church of France, opposing the Pope, persecuting the Jansenists and, more particularly, the Protestants, and finally revoking the Edict of Nantes in 1685. As a result, thousands of Protestants fled the country. Louis XIV acted as a patron of the Arts and both the arts and letters flourished thanks to the patronage afforded by the king to many artists, the creation of academies and the many buildings commissioned by him. He was married to Maria-Theresa in whom he quickly lost interest. He had many mistresses and countless children, all of whom he legitimised. After the Queen's death in 1683, the king secretly remarried. His second wife was Madame de Maintenon.

The façade overlooking the gardens, completed by Jules Hardouin-Mansart in 1689. Palace of Versailles (Yvelines).

The Revolution and the Empire

French Revolution

1789 : 5th May, meeting of the States General in Versailles. Oath taken in the real tennis court (20th June).
14th July: storming of the Bastille by the people of Paris.
July-August: the "Great Fear" in rural areas.
4th August: the Constituent Assembly abolishes privileges. The "night of 4th August".
26th August: Vote on the Declaration of the Rights of Man and of the Citizen.

1790 : Creation of départements. Voting in of the civil constitution for the clergy.

1791 : 20th-21st June: the royal family flees but is recaptured in Varennes.
1st October: establishment of a constitutional monarchy with Louis XVI.

1792 : 20th April: France declares war on Austria.
10th August: fall of Louis XVI. The Republic is proclaimed on 21st September.
20th September: French forces win the Battle of Valmy.

1793 : 21st January: execution of King Louis XVI.
February-March: the first anti-French coalition is formed.
10th March: uprising in Vendée (ÿ March 1796). The Revolutionary Tribunal is set up.
31st May-2nd June: Fall of the Girondins. The Montagnards take power.
13th July: Charlotte Corday murders Marat.

1794 : 5th April: execution of Danton.
June: Robespierre institutes a "dictatorship". He is overthrown and guillotined on 28th July.
26th June: France defeats Austria at the Battle of Fleurus.

1795 : 26th October: beginning of the Directory.
The French forces conquer the Low Countries and annex Belgium.

1796-1797 : Bonaparte's Italian campaign (victories at Arcole and Rivoli).
Treaty of Campo-Formio signed with Austria (1797).

1798 : January-February: French forces capture Rome and set up the Roman Republic.
July: start of Bonaparte's Egyptian expedition (ÿ August 1799).
5th September: Jourdan Law on conscription.
September: the second anti-French coalition is formed.

Consulate

1799 : 9th-10th November: Bonaparte implements a coup d'état and becomes First Consul. He pro claims himself consul for life on 4th August 1802.

1800 : 13th February: creation of the Banque de France.
17th February: nomination of the first Prefects.
14th June: the French defeat the Austrians at the Battle of Marengo. The Treaty of Lunéville is signed in 1801.

1801 : Signature of the concordat between Bonaparte and Pope Pius VII.

1802 : Signature of the Treaty of Amiens with England. General peace (ÿ May 1803).
Reorganisation of secondary schooling and opening of high schools.
Creation of the Legion of Honour.

1803 : 28th March: Creation of the franc germinal.

Château de Malmaison, Rueil-Malmaison, Hauts-de-Seine. ▼

The Bonaparte dynasty

Charles-Marie Bonaparte (1746-1785) — m. 1764 Maria Letizia Ramolino (1750-1836)

- **Joseph Bonaparte** (1768-1844) King of Naples (1806-1808) King of Spain (1808-1813)
- **NAPOLEON I** (1769-1821) Emperor of the French People (1804-1814 and in 1815)
  - m. 1796 Joséphine de Beauharnais (1763-1814)
  - m. 1810 Marie-Louise (1791-1847) daughter of the Emperor of Austria
    - **Napoléon II** (1811-1832) King of Rome Duc de Reichstadt
- **Louis Bonaparte** (1778-1846) King of Holland (1806-1810) — m. 1802 Hortense de Beauharnais (1783-1837)
  - **NAPOLÉON III** (1808-1873) Emperor of the French People (1852-1870) — m. 1853 Eugénie de Montijo (1826-1920)
    - **Eugène Louis Napoléon Bonaparte** (1856-1879) Prince Imperial
- **Jérôme Bonaparte** (1784-1860) King of Westphalia (1807-1813)

Napoléon Bonaparte, 1769-1821. ▶

Empire

1804 : Promulgation of the Civil Code.
18th May: the Empire is established and Bonaparte becomes Napoleon I.

1805 : The third anti-French coalition is set up
(defeat at Trafalgar on 21st October, victory at Austerlitz on 2nd December).

1806 : The fourth anti-French coalition is set up (French victories at Jena and Auerstadt on 14th October; victories at Eylau on 8th February 1807 and Friedland on 14th June 1807).
Implementation of the Continental Blockade.

1807 : Treaties of Tilsitt signed with Russia.
Start of the conquest of Portugal by the French who evacuate their troops in 1811.

1808 : Joseph Bonaparte is King of Spain. Popular uprising (ÿ 1813).

1809 : Formation of the fifth anti-French coalition (French victories at Eckmühl on 22nd April and Wagram on 6th July).
16th December: divorce of Napoleon I and Josephine de Beauharnais.
Napoleon remarries with Marie-Louise of Austria on 2nd April 1810.

1810 : Promulgation of the Criminal Code.
The Low Countries are annexed to France.

1812 : Napoleon I's Russian campaign ends in disaster at the crossing of the Beresina River.

1813 : Sixth anti-French coalition (the French are defeated at Leipzig on 19th October).

1814 : Invasion of France. Napoleon abdicates on 6th April. Louis XVIII becomes King of France.

1815 : Napoleon I returns to power for the period known as the "One Hundred Days" (20th March-22nd June).
He is defeated at Waterloo on 18th June and abdicates for the second time. He is exiled on St. Helena.

Portrait of Napoleon. ▲

A close-up of a fountain ("Le Palmier") in Paris. ▲

Napoleon (1769-1821) – Emperor of the French People (1804-1814 and 1815)

Napoleon Bonaparte, who was born in Corsica, underwent military training then joined the revolutionary army. Having distinguished himself on several occasions between 1793 and 1795, he was put in charge of the Italian campaign and proved himself to be a great war leader in the face of attack from the Austrians (1796-1797). The Egyptian expedition brought him lasting popularity (1798-1799). In October 1799, he returned to France where the Directory was facing enormous difficulties. Bonaparte organised a coup d'état with Sieyès (November 1799) and instigated the Consulate. He obtained widesweeping powers that enabled him to pacify and reorganise the country (signature of the Concordat, implementation of the Prefect system, creation of the Banque de France and the franc germinal, promulgation of the Civil Code). Outside France, wars instigated by revolutionaries continued. Bonaparte succeeded in re-establishing a general peace in 1802. He took advantage of this to strengthen his power and had himself appointed consul for life (August 1802) before turning the country into an Empire (18th May 1804). He became the Emperor of the French People under the name Napoleon I. This marked a return to a hereditary monarchical regime which became increasingly authoritarian (suppression of individual liberties, assemblies with no real power, education under tight control). The population did not react; it was closely monitored by an ever-present police force. Napoleon was, however, supported by the French as long as he won military victories. He succeeded in overthrowing the third coalition thanks to his defeat of the Austrians at Austerlitz (1805). When confronted with the fourth coalition, Napoleon defeated Prussia (1806) then Russia which was forced to accept the French alliance (Treaty of Tilsitt, 1807). England stood alone, at war. In order to asphyxiate the enemy's economy, Napoleon instituted the Continental Blockade (1806) but this obliged him to invade Spain and Portugal (1806-1807). When Austria saw the difficulties facing the French in the Iberian Peninsula, it took up arms again but was defeated at Wagram (1809) and had to ally itself to France. The annexation of the Low Countries in 1810 and the North of Germany in 1811 gave the country greater territorial expansion than it had ever known. This marked the peak of the Napoleonic Empire's success. However, the absence of civil liberties and the economic and financial consequences of the war eventually created general discontent. In Europe, the defeated countries began to rise from the ashes. In 1812, France broke off relations with Russia and Napoleon launched a new campaign which ended in a veritable débâcle when his army crossed back across the River Beresina. After the defeat, all the countries in Europe rose to combat France and a sixth coalition was formed (1813). Napoleon was initially victorious in battle but was then defeated in Leipzig and this led to the invasion of France. The coalition forces reached Paris by March 1814 and the Emperor was forced to abdicate. He was exiled to the island of Elba; Louis XVIII mounted the throne of France. However, less than one year later, Napoleon returned to France by stealth and seized power again (the "One Hundred Days"). His European enemies then formed a coalition that resulted in the French defeat at Waterloo (1815). Napoleon I abdicated for a second time and the British deported him to St. Helena where he died in 1821.en 1821.

Napoleon III

1815 to 1914

1815 :	King Louis XVIII mounts the throne. Election of the "Incomparable Chamber".
1820 :	Assassination of the Duc de Berry, Louis XVIII's nephew. Laws are passed to restrict individual liberties, the freedom of the press and universal suffrage.
1822 :	Execution of the "four sergeants of La Rochelle" on grounds on treason.
1824 :	Death of Louis XVIII. He is succeeded by his brother, Charles X.
1825 :	The Chamber votes in the "billion francs for émigrés" law compensating émigrés for property lost during the Revolution.
1827 :	Opponents of the government are victorious in the general election.
1828 :	Liberal law on the press.
1830 :	Revolution in Paris: the "Three Glorious Days" (27th-28th-29th July). King Charles X abdicates. Louis-Philippe I becomes King of the French People, the "Citizen King". The French capture Algiers.
1831 :	Silk workers' revolt in Lyon.
c. 1840 :	Start of the Industrial Revolution.
1848 :	Revolution in Paris (22nd-24th February). King Louis-Philippe I abdicates and the Republic is proclaimed. Freedom of expression and universal suffrage are re-established. The working day is limited. Slavery is abolished in the colonies. 10th December: Louis-Napoleon Bonaparte is elected President of the Republic.
1850 :	The Falloux Law on education is passed.
1851 :	2nd December: coup d'état by Louis-Napoleon Bonaparte.
1852 :	2nd December: proclamation of the Empire. Louis-Napoleon Bonaparte becomes Napoleon III.
1853 :	Baron Haussmann is appointed Prefect of Seine.
1854-1856 :	Crimean War against Russia, in support of the Ottoman Empire.
1859 :	Italian Campaign against Austria. The French army is victorious at Magenta and Solferino.
1860 :	Signature of a free trade treaty with Great Britain. Savoy and Nice are annexed to France.
1862 :	French expedition to Mexico (ÿ 1867).
1864 :	A law is passed authorising workers' coalitions and granting the right to strike.

In 1820, Louis XVIII presents his grand-nephew, the Duc de Bordeaux, son of the Duc de Berry who had been assassinated a few months earlier. Château de Chambord (Loir-et-Cher).

3rd Republic / Second Empire

1868 :	Niel Law re-organising the army. Liberal law on the press. Law granting freedom of assembly.
1870 :	21st May: Napoleon III sets up a liberal Empire. July: outbreak of war against Prussia. French defeats in August. Napoleon III capitulates. The Republic is proclaimed on 4th September.
1871 :	17th February: Thiers becomes leader of the executive then President of the Republic on 31st August. March-May: Paris Commune. 10th May: Treaty of Frankfurt signed with Prussia. France loses Alsace and Lorraine.
1872 :	Law on military recruitment laying the basis for mandatory five-year military service.
1873 :	Thiers resigns. Maréchal de Mac-Mahon is elected President of the Republic. Failed attempt at restoring the monarchy with the Comte de Chambord.
c. 1873-1896 :	"Great Depression", a period of economic and social crisis.
1875 :	Votes on constitutional laws establishing the Third Republic.
1879 :	Mac-Mahon resigns and July Grévy is elected President of the Republic.
1879-1882 :	Laws are passed setting up mandatory civic education.
1884 :	The Waldeck-Rousseau Law authorises trades unions.
1888-1889 :	Boulanger crisis.
1889 :	World Fair in Paris. Construction of the Eiffel Tower.
1894 :	Beginning of the Dreyfus affair. Dreyfus receives a presidential pardon in 1899.
1899 :	Formation of the Waldeck-Rousseau government of "Republican Defence".
1901 :	A law is passed on non profit-making associations.
1902 :	A general election results in victory for left-wing parties. Emile Combes implements anticlerical policies.
1905 :	A law is passed separating Church and State.
1906 :	Georges Clémenceau becomes head of the government.
1911 :	Franco-German crisis centring on Morocco.
1914 :	28th June: assassination of Franz Ferdinand, heir to the throne of Austria-Hungary in Sarajevo. 31st July: assassination of Jean Jaurès.

Palais du Trocadéro built by Davioud in the late 19th century and replaced, in 1937, by the Palais de Chaillot in Paris. ▼

Post-1914

Gare de l'Est (Paris) at the beginning of the 20th century. ▸

Third Republic

1914 : 3rd August: outbreak of the First World War. Trench warfare from November onwards.
1916 : February-June: Battle of Verdun.
1917 : 2nd April: The USA enters the war.
15th May: Pétain becomes chief of the French armed forces and ends the mutinies.
16th November: Clémenceau forms a government.
1918 : 26th March : Foch becomes Commander-in-Chief of the allied forces.
11th November: Signature of the Armistice at Réthondes. End of the First World War.
1919 : 28th June: Signature of the Treaty of Versailles with Germany.
1920 : December: founding of the Communist Party.
1924 : May: Herriot government. Financial crisis and speculation against the franc.
1926 : July: Poincaré becomes President of the Council and stabilises the franc.
1931 : France is affected by the global economic slump.
1934 : January: anti-parliamentarian feeling is rife after the Stavisky affair. A riot on 6th February leads to the formation of the Doumergue government of "National Unity".
1936 : April-May: General election with victory for the Popular Front. Léon Blum becomes head of the government. Social laws are passed (paid annual holidays, 40-hour working week).
1938 : 29th-30th September: Daladier, head of the government, signs the Munich Accords with Hitler.
1939 : 3rd September: outbreak of the Second World War.
1940 : 10th May: German invasion. The French suffer defeats. Pétain signs the armistice on 22nd June.
18th June: call to resistance from General de Gaulle in London.
10th July: beginning of the Vichy regime under Maréchal Pétain.
3rd October: the Vichy regime promulgates the law on the status of Jews.
1941 : The French Volunteer Legion (L.V.F.) is set up to fight bolshevism.
1942 : 16th-17th July: Jews are rounded up in Paris and taken to the "Vel d'hiv" sports stadium.
8th November: Allied landing in North Africa. The Germans invade the free zone.
1943 : 30th January: the Militia is set up.
16th February: Mandatory work service (S.T.O.) is introduced.
27th May: Jean Moulin sets up the National Council of the Resistance (C.N.R.).

Palais de Chaillot built for the 1937 World Fair (Paris). ▲

Fourth Republic

Fifth Republic

1944 : 6th June: Allied landing in Normandy. A further landing takes place in Provence on 15th August.
10th June: The Germans massacre the population of Oradour-sur-Glane.
25th August: Paris is liberated. De Gaulle takes power.
5th October: French women are given the vote.

1944-1946 : Companies are nationalised in several sectors of the economy.

1945 : 8th May: The Germans surrender. End of the Second World War in Europe.

1946 : 20th January: General de Gaulle resigns from the head of the provisional government.

1947 : January: beginning of the Fourth Republic. Vincent Auriol is elected President of the Republic.
June: France accepts the American Marshall Plan.

1949 : France becomes a member of NATO.

1951 : 18th April: Treaty of Paris setting up the European Coal and Steel Community (E.C.S.C.).

1953 : 23rd December: René Coty is elected President of the Republic.

1954 : 7th May: French defeat in Dien Bien Phu. Indo-China gains independence (21st July).
17th June: a government is formed under Pierre Mendès-France.
1st November: revolt in Algeria.

1956 : 2nd January: a general election brings victory to the "Republican Front". Guy Mollet becomes head of the government.
March: independence of Morocco and Tunisia.
November-December: Franco-British military intervention in Suez.

1957 : 25th March: Treaty of Rome setting up the European Economic Community (E.E.C.).

1958 : 13th May: military leaders seize power in Algiers. De Gaulle becomes President of the Council on 31st May.

1959 : 8th January: de Gaulle becomes President of the Republic. Beginning of the Fifth Republic.

1960 : 1st January: the new franc becomes legal tender.
January-November: independence is granted to 14 French colonies in Africa.
13th February: France's first atomic explosion in Reggane, in the Sahara.

1961 : April: the "Generals' Putsch" in Algiers.

1962 : 18th March: signature of the Evian Accords. Algeria becomes independent on 3rd July. Mass exodus of Algerians of French descent (the "pieds-noirs").
22nd August: terrorist attack on De Gaulle at Le Petit-Clamart.
28th October: a referendum approves a project aimed at the election of the President of the Republic by universal suffrage.

1965 : December: De Gaulle is re-elected.

1966 : July: France withdraws from NATO.

1968 : May: student crisis and social unrest.

1969 : April: De Gaulle resigns after the failure of his referendum. Pompidou succeeds him in June.
1973 : First "oil crisis". Start of an economic crisis in 1974.
1974 : 2nd April: death of President Pompidou. Giscard d'Estaing is elected in May.
June: the age of majority is reduced to 18 years.
1975 : 17th January: promulgation of the Veil Law authorising abortion.
1979 : March: the European Monetary System is implemented.
24th December: first launch of the Ariane European space rocket.
Start of the second "oil crisis". The economic situation declines.
1981 : 10th May: Mitterrand is elected President of the Republic. The left-wing government passes numerous social laws (retirement at 60, 39-hour working week, 5th week of annual paid holi days), nationalises a number of companies and implements decentralisation measures.
September: Parliament abolishes the death penalty.
1986 : January-March: slump in oil prices. Start of the "counter-oil crisis".
16th March: a general election gives victory to the right wing. Jacques Chirac becomes Prime Minister.
1988 : 8th May: President Mitterrand is re-elected.
12th October: a law is passed setting up a minimum reinsertion benefit (R.M.I.).
1991 : 17th January-28th February: the French army is involved in the Gulf War.
October-Nov. : start of the scandal surrounding the supply of blood contaminated by the AIDS virus in 1985.
1992 : 20th September: the Treaty of Maastricht is approved by referendum.
1993 : 1st January: the Single European Market comes into effect among the twelve EEC countries.
March: a general election gives victory to the right wing. Edouard Balladur is Prime Minister.
1st November: The Treaty of Maastricht comes into effect.
1995 : 7th May: Jacques Chirac is elected President of the Republic.
1996 : 28th May: President Chirac announces that military service will be discontinued in 1997.
1997 : May-June: an early general election gives victory to the left wing. Lionel Jospin becomes Prime Minister.
8th October: Papon is tried for crimes against humanity.
1998 : 17th March: promulgation of the law reforming access to French nationality.
8th April: a law is passed on the entry and residence of foreigners.
19th May: a law is passed decreasing the legal working week to 35 hours.
1999 : 1st January: the single European currency, the Euro, comes into effect.
24th March-10th June: French troops are involved in NATO military intervention in Kosovo.
26th-28th December: two violent storms ravage the country.

6th June 1944, Allied landings in Normandy. There was fierce fighting before the German forces surrendered. ▼

The radome in Pleumeur-Bodou, site of the first intercontinental television satellite link-up on 11th July 1962 (Côtes d'Armor)

Charles de Gaulle (1890-1970) – General and Politician

After military studies at Saint-Cyr, de Gaulle took part in the First World War. In the interwar years, he joined Pétain's office at the High Council for War (1925-1927) before being appointed to the Secretariat of the High Council for National Defence (1931-1938). De Gaulle was a military theorist who published numerous works in which he supported a war of movement. During the German invasion of 1940, after a few victories, he was appointed Under-Secretary of State at the National Defence Office by the head of government, Paul Reynaud. He was in favour of continuing the war and opposed supporters of the armistice. When the Pétain government was set up, he left France for London from which he launched a call to resistance (18th June). De Gaulle then organised "Free France", received the support of French soldiers, rallied the African colonies and recreated an army. He made contact with the French Underground through Jean Moulin who set up the National Council for Resistance in 1943. In June 1944, De Gaulle founded the Provisional Government of the French Republic. After the Allied landing in Normandy and the liberation of France, he came to Paris (August 1944) and rose to power. He launched the reconstruction of the country but quickly came into conflict with the political parties on the question of future institutions. He resigned in January 1946. He then opposed the Fourth Republic and founded the R.P.F. (1947) but the party was unable to impose itself as an opposition group. De Gaulle found himself "out on a limb".

The Algerian crisis enabled him to return to power. After the putsch in Algiers (13th May 1958), he was seen as the only man capable of redressing the situation. He became plenipotentiary President of the Council with authority to draft a new Constitution. De Gaulle then founded the Fifth Republic and became its first President (1959-1969). Granted wide-ranging powers, he left his mark on French political life. He gave priority to economic growth by launching the Pinay-Rueff Plan then undertaking structural reforms that allowed for the strong economic development of the 1960's. He settled colonial problems by granting independence to countries in Black Africa (1960) then, after a difficult, controversial process, to Algeria (1962). In foreign affairs, de Gaulle took national independence as his credo and this led him into dispute with the USA (French withdrawal from NATO in 1966) and the EEC, while taking France closer to the Communist block and the Third World. After modifying the Constitution (1962) in order to allow for presidential election by universal suffrage, de Gaulle was re-elected in 1965 but Gaullism had already begun its decline. His majority only scraped through in the 1967 general election. His political longevity, advancing years and authoritarian behaviour were beginning to tire people. Social, economic and financial difficulties arose. The rejection of Gaullism was crystallised in the May 1968 student revolt, social unrest and political crisis. Although de Gaulle succeeded in redressing the situation, his power base appeared shaken. He sought to regain the upper hand and organised a referendum on the reform of the Senate and regionalisation. The negative result led to his resignation in 1969.

 - Imprimé et façonné par Pollina à Luçon n° L95147 - Photogravure d'Aquitaine à Bordeaux - Imprimé en France